D0582105

Calm the Soul

A Book of Simple Wisdom and Prayer

The illustrations in the book come from The Poor Clares, Galway.
The illustration used throughout is of the monastery in
Nuns' Island, Galway, and others feature: San Damiano, Assisi,
the first monastery of The Order of St Clare; Bethlehem, Athlone,
the original monastery of the Galway Poor Clares;
and Galway Cathedral.

Calm the Soul
A Book of Simple Wisdom and Prayer

The Poor Clares, Galway

HACHETTE
BOOKS
IRELAND

First published in Ireland in 2012 by Hachette Books Ireland
A Hachette UK company

1

Copyright © The Poor Clares, Galway

The right of The Poor Clares, Galway to be identified as the Author of the
Work has been asserted by them in accordance with the Copyright,
Designs and Patents Act 1988.

A CIP catalogue record for this title is available from the British Library.

ISBN 978 1444 743760

Typeset in Centabel Book and Carolingia by Solutions 2d.

Printed and bound by Clays Ltd, St Ives plc

Hachette Books Ireland policy is to use papers that are natural, renewable
and recyclable products and made from wood grown in sustainable
forests. The logging and manufacturing processes are expected to conform
to the environmental regulations of the country of origin.

Hachette Books Ireland
8 Castlecourt Centre
Castleknock
Dublin 15
www.hachette.ie

A division of
Hachette UK
338 Euston Road
London NW1 3BH

Contents

Calm the Soul

When my boat, Lord, is storm tossed and sinking,
When fears in my heart take control,
Say 'Be not afraid' to my spirit,
And Your answer will calm the soul.

When I flounder around in deep waters,
When the stresses of life take their toll,
A sudden deep hush steals upon me,
Your gentleness calms the soul.

When my life seems full of confusion
And I have lost sight of the goal,
As I stumble about in the darkness
May Your gentle light calm the soul.

I often live life on the surface,
Sometimes I'm playing a role,
Help me cherish my own inner beauty,
May Your tender love calm the soul.

When sinfulness tugs like an anchor,
When guilt has me caught in a hole.
I turn to You Lord for forgiveness,
And Your mercy calms the soul.

When I struggle with sickness and sorrow,
And eagerly long to be whole,
I call on Your name to bring healing
And the touch of Your hand calms the soul.

Introduction

Another book on prayer? It seems that there are so many as it is – why bring out another? Well, circumstances change and time stands still for no one. There have been phenomenal changes in the past decade and we now live in a very different world, an extremely busy world. The reality is that, today, people are trying to juggle more and more activities in their day-to-day lives – earning a living, looking after children and homes, and studying, to name but a few. Advances in technology and the way we communicate have brought with them incessant demands for our attention.

We seek serenity of heart, but find that there is no space given for our souls. Silence is all but gone and, yet, silence itself can be healing. Allied to this is the reality that for many people, the pace of life has increased greatly. A rushed quality pervades our world and can rob us of peace. Living constantly on a treadmill, it is hard to appreciate how much our energy can be depleted through continued rushing. The result is that there is a high level of unease.

God wants us to live at peace, to have serenity and harmony in our hearts, but, today, these things can be difficult to find. Sometimes the importance of the spiritual

aspect of life is not appreciated, and from what people have told us, by post or when they visit the monastery, there's a real hunger for some tranquillity and silence. Despite the great changes that have occurred in our world, human nature is still the same, with the same needs.

The prayers and reflections in this book began on our website as a way to present ideas about prayer to people with busy, changing lives. Blessed John Paul II asked Christian communities to become 'schools of prayer'. In this book we have brought together the fruits of our own prayer life to offer simple ideas on prayer in straight-forward, bite-sized portions.

As St Clare was the first female follower of St Francis, this book is permeated with a Franciscan flavour. The primary concern at prayer for both St Clare and St Francis, as in all of life, was the '*Spirit of the Lord and His holy activity*'. This was the guiding force in their lives and if you were to ask them about prayer methods, they would probably recommend that you follow the lead of the Holy Spirit rather than force yourself into any particular method of prayer. The Holy Spirit leads each one of us in a different manner. That is the freedom and beauty of Franciscan prayer and is the essence we draw upon in this book.

Everyone is different and there is no such thing as the perfect way to pray. The important thing is to be open to the Holy Spirit and to allow yourself to be led in prayer. Because we are all individuals, each of the ways of prayer in this book can be applied in different ways and will speak to each individual soul in a unique way.

When Jesus said, '*You must come away to some lonely place all by yourselves and rest for a while*' (Mark 6:31), it was an invitation to give ourselves a chance to have our batteries recharged and be refreshed by His grace. Our prayer is that the simple ideas, prayers and reflections we have collated here will help to calm the souls of those who read them and will help each of you as you respond to the deep hunger for God which is written into every human heart.

St Clare

A Woman for Our Times

Clare Offreduccio, whom we know as St Clare of Assisi, may seem like a remote medieval figure. What could such a woman, who lived most of her life locked up in a monastery in Assisi in the thirteenth century, have to say to those of us living in this age of social media? What relevance could her life have for those of us living at the dawn of the third millennium?

St Clare was the first female follower of St Francis of Assisi, and she has lived in his shadow for many years. However, she was no shrinking violet locked up in an ivory tower and unaware of the realities of life. As someone who had to fight to achieve what she felt was necessary, she has much to say to us.

Living at a time when women had little or no say in the way their lives were shaped, she emerged as a woman who lived her life in a resolute and passionate way, and who let nothing stop her from living out her vision of life as it began to unfold before her. She came under the influence of St Francis, having often heard him preach, and she met with him many times. This had to be done in secret because she was from a noble family, and they would certainly not have approved of her associating with such a strange man.

But she could not keep away because, in the words of her contemporary biographer, St Francis' words *'seemed to her, afire with God'* and it became clear to her that she was being called to embark on a new way of living with the Lord.

Leaving aside all security, she secretly left home on the night of Palm Sunday 1212 to join St Francis and his followers. It is hard for us today to imagine how shocking this must have been – a young, beautiful girl of eighteen going off on her own with a band of ragamuffin friars. However, she was single-minded and passionately in love with the Lord, and would not let anything stand in her way. When she later counselled that we should *'totally love Him who gave Himself totally for your love'* (3 LAg 15), she was clearly speaking from experience.

Life was difficult in those early years. Originally, there was no specific monastery for St Clare to stay in but, eventually, she moved into San Damiano, one of the old churches that St Francis had repaired. Not long after she left home, she was joined by her younger sister Agnes and, eventually, many other women joined her (even her mother) – and so the Poor Clares began.

As leader of this group of women, St Clare had to be firm in her resolve to secure permission to live a radically poor way of life. In those days, it was unheard of for monasteries of women to live without land or revenue to support them. However, St Clare wanted to embrace the Poor Crucified Christ in a radical way, and so she appealed to the pope in order to secure the *privilege of poverty* (to have no possessions whatsoever). Although highly thought of by three popes, each was very reluctant to grant this privilege to her. However, St Clare's conviction about poverty was crucial to her vision of life. Someone who lives in poverty is dependent on God and gives a clear testimony to her trust in Him.

She was also the first woman in Church history to write a rule of life for religious women and to get it approved. This was also something very close to her heart, as several different religious rules had been proposed for her community, none of which reflected the Franciscan ideal that she wanted to live. So, she set about writing her own 'Form of Life', which was approved by Pope Innocent IV the day before she died as she lay on her deathbed! Two years later, in 1255, her name was enrolled among the saints.

Such then was St Clare of Assisi – a woman of passion, courage and determination, with an all-consuming love for the Lord. Yet she was very gentle and considerate in her nature, something that is borne out by the testimonies of her sisters and also her rule, which is noted for these traits. Down through the years, the noble and austere way of life she founded has never ceased to inspire and attract women who have the generosity and love to follow it.

Preparing
for Prayer

Why Pray?

Prayer is the food of the soul. Just as our bodies need nourishment, so, too, do our souls, which, in hungering for God, need to be nourished by prayer. Much of the stress that many people experience today comes from the fact that they neglect to nourish their souls. Our bodies, minds and souls make up a unit. Our society is becoming more and more geared towards looking after the body and the mind, but unless some harmony is restored by including the soul and bringing these three elements together, it is inevitable that people will experience anxiety. St Augustine said, '*You have made us for Yourself and our hearts are restless until they rest in You.*' We believe that a lot of the anxiety that people experience in their busy lives could be alleviated if they gave some time to prayer and the search for God. Jesus is the Source of Peace and we cannot hope to have peace within ourselves unless we draw life from that source.

Essentially, prayer is a conversation with God, speaking to Him who created and loves us and listening to what He has to say to us. In this book, we want to offer a few

different methods of prayer that we feel are well suited to the type of lives we live today. Prayer is a relationship, so we all experience it differently. We have given examples of different types of prayer and hope that you will find an approach that suits you. Why not decide to spend ten or fifteen minutes a day in prayer? If you already do this, why not increase it to thirty minutes?

Prayer and holiness is for everyone in every situation. It is having our whole being in harmony with God's plan for us. We will never achieve true happiness if we continue to search for it outside the very source of love, which we know is God Himself. Scripture tells us that '*God is love*' (1 John 4:16).

As the Blessed John Paul II said in his letter on the dawn of the new millennium, why not '*start afresh from Christ*'? You won't regret it!

How to Pray

Jesus tells us that, when you pray, you should '*go to your private room and, when you have shut your door, pray to your Father who is in that secret place, and your Father who sees all that is done in secret will reward you*' (Matthew 6:6). It is important that when we come to pray we give the Lord 'quality time'. Our prayer is a relationship, so we need to work on it.

One does not pray only when one has the time.
One makes time for the Lord.

CCC 2710

We are human and prone to distractions, so we should avail of whatever supports to prayer are available. Try creating a suitable atmosphere, a quiet room, perhaps with candles and soft music. It is not necessary to have a set place for prayer, but it can be helpful. Sometimes, you may be able to visit a chapel. This has the added advantage that if the Blessed Sacrament is there, you are actually in His sacramental presence. You should always begin with a prayer to the Holy Spirit, to help you to be open to His inspirations. Scripture says, '*The Spirit too*

comes to help us in our weakness. For when we cannot choose words in order to pray properly, the Spirit Himself expresses our plea in a way that could never be put into words' (Romans 8:26).

We could ask for His help in our own words or use a simple invocation such as '*Come, Holy Spirit*'. We can also use this beautiful prayer by Cardinal Mercier.

O Holy Spirit, soul of my soul
I adore you.
Enlighten me, guide me,
Strengthen me and console me.
Tell me what I ought to do
And command me to do it
I promise to be submissive in everything
That you ask me to do
And to accept everything that you permit
To happen to me.
Only show me what is your will
And give me the grace to do it.
Amen.

When we begin to pray, it is important that we become conscious that God is love and He loves us passionately.

All our prayer is a response to the God who loved us first. God's love for us is a free gift, it is gratuitous. We don't have to earn this love. He loves you as you are right now. As you come to pray, listen to Him speaking words of love in Scripture and realise that they are addressed to you personally. As you hear God speak, allow the reality of His love for you to penetrate your heart. '*I have loved you with an everlasting love. I still maintain my faithful love for you*' (Jeremiah 31:3).

There is a story from our Franciscan tradition that one night St Francis went through the forest, weeping because '*Love is not loved*'. He was deeply aware that God is Love and he found it heartbreaking that so many people ignored God. He lived his life as a response to that love. St Clare's response was '*totally love Him who gave Himself totally for your love*'. Our journey, too, is to reciprocate that love.

Always remember
God has called you into being
God loves you more than
you can ever imagine
God has a vital purpose for your life.

Silence

There is a real need for us to learn to appreciate the value of silence. The widespread use of technology impinges on us, maybe more than we realise. There always seems to be some level of noise. Though we may not fully be aware of how much it is affecting us, it has an impact. Even subtle 'white noise' in the background has an effect. While it may seem innocuous enough, we often feel drained by it, and it seems like we can't hear ourselves think. Our senses can become overwhelmed. Noise contributes to us having difficulty sleeping, as our minds try to process everything with which we have been bombarded during the day. And then we wonder why our nerves are frayed and we are frazzled at the end of the day!

Silence is little respected today and yet it is essential for a healthy life and for prayer. Silence has so many benefits. It is like a blanket we wrap around ourselves to enable us to sink deeper into the true reality of life and into our being. When the very atmosphere possesses a profound peace and tranquillity, it lends itself to a gentler approach to living. It gives us a better capacity to listen both to others and to God. It helps to drain away stress and tension and can bring with it a sense of calmness. We all know that silence is very important for meditation – vital in fact; the word of God penetrates more deeply when we have both outward and inward silence.

In music, we need both notes and rests – sound and the silence unite to produce a harmonious blend. This is a perfect analogy for our lives. Speech is good, but we also need to give time to open up these spaces of quiet in order to bring about harmony in our lives.

Silence can be challenging. While it is beneficial, it can also be painful, because it provides a space for the things that we have buried to surface. If this happens, the silence can also provide a forum in which we can bring these issues to the Lord and ask Him to heal us. We often live disconnected from our inner selves because we may have suppressed things that we do not like about ourselves. We need to let these things surface, and allow them to be healed and integrated. As each memory is awakened, we simply try to hand it over to the Lord for healing, for we read, '*Unload all your worries on to Him, for He is looking after you*' (1 Peter 5:7). See the recommendations in the 'On Healing' section in the Further Reading and Reflections chapter.

When we enter an undisturbed silence, we can be more attentive to the truth of who we are. It also provides an ambiance in which the Word of God can be received and cherished. While silence of itself is not prayer, it helps create an atmosphere conducive to prayer. To allow the Word of God to work on us, we need to let it penetrate our souls. We must allow our souls to become tranquil. Then, like drops of water sinking into a still pond, we let the ripples go forth, gently touching the deepest recesses of our hearts. Let the sound of these words of the Lord echo and re-echo within you and find a home there.

Ways to Pray

Intercession and Petition

We are usually fairly good at the 'asking' type of prayer – it comes naturally to us when things go wrong or we are out of our depth. God is our loving Father who is anxious to provide for us and loves when we turn to Him in prayer. Intercession is possibly our most instinctive way of praying, and Scripture invites us to pray this way when Jesus says, '*Ask and you shall receive*' (Matthew 7:7). However, God also wants us to come to know Him and the fullness of His love for us.

We are told many things about this type of prayer. For example, '*If you find your delight in the Lord, He will grant you your heart's desire*' (Psalm 36/37:4). This is very similar to what Jesus tells us: '*Set your hearts on his kingdom first, and on his righteousness, and all these other things will be given you as well*' (Matthew 6:33). This means that when we come to intercede, we should look to the Lord and His righteousness first, to delight in His company and then to ask for what we need. It means that we do not take God for granted – and this makes sense, when we remember that the Lord wants us to enter into relationship with Him.

The way that Jesus interceded is an example for us. We often find that before He performed a miracle, He blessed God first. For example, before He raised Lazarus from the dead, He turned in thanksgiving to the Father (John 11:41–42). We also find Him blessing the bread before the multiplication of the loaves (Luke 9:15–16).

The 'Our Father' is a perfect example of this type of prayer. Here, the first three petitions are devoted to praise of the Father and praying for His will – only then do we move on to intercession as such.

Scripture also tells us, '*If two of you on earth agree to ask anything at all, it will be granted to you by my Father in heaven*' (Matthew 18:19). There is incredible power in unity of hearts at prayer, because God is the source of all unity.

One of the incidents from the life of St Clare that illustrates her style of intercession profoundly was when the sisters' monastery (which lay just outside the city of Assisi) was threatened by Saracen troops. Not only were they in mortal danger, but so, too, was the city as the soldiers were on the way to attack it. St Clare was bed-ridden, but the sisters came to her in crisis. She asked them to bring her to the door of the monastery and then asked for the pyx, containing the Blessed Sacrament, to be brought out too.

Though she was sick, St Clare prostrated herself before the Lord in prayer, an act of profound worship. Then, holding the Blessed Sacrament aloft, she begged Him to defend her sisters, whom she could not defend. A voice, like that of a little child, was heard and it said, '*I will always defend you.*' Clare continued to pray, saying, '*My Lord, please protect this city which for Your love sustains us.*' This incident, perhaps more than any other, shows St Clare's great devotion to and trust in the Eucharist. It is why she is usually depicted with the Blessed Sacrament in a monstrance.

21

Praying in the Spirit of St Clare

St Clare fell passionately in love with Christ. She had a distinct relationship with each person of the Holy Trinity – Father, Son and Holy Spirit – however, she focused her eyes and her affections on Christ, whom she said had become for us 'the Way'. With this love, she was able to face the trials that came her way. She was courageous and determined. She grew in understanding and became a very balanced person, which can be seen clearly in her writing. For both St Clare and St Francis, everyone was a brother or sister: all were treated the same. Everyone and everything was a gift, and their lives and spirituality were characterised by gratitude.

St Clare wrote no treatises on prayer. However, her letters to St Agnes of Prague form the central part of her writings and give us a marvellous insight into what animated her heart. St Agnes was a princess from Bohemia who had been much sought after in marriage, even by Emperor Frederick II. However, Christ had captured her heart and she resolved to give herself completely to Him. When she heard of the way of life

that St Clare and her sisters were following, she was attracted to what they were doing. She established a Poor Clare convent in Prague and began a correspondence with St Clare. Four of the letters survive and they are very important for helping us to appreciate St Clare's vision of life.

The letters provide a window into the soul of St Clare. They are less formal than the rule and in them we can see the progression in both St Clare's spirituality, as her prayer life matured and developed, and her deepening friendship with St Agnes. The letters show her as a very affectionate woman, capable of deep friendship and not afraid to express her affection openly. They also reveal her clarity of vision and her ability to home in on the essentials of life and living. These she articulated in a way that inspired St Agnes and those who have followed her down through the centuries. Their value is incalculable.

In the letters, you can detect the concern of a mother for her spiritual daughter, that she learn to know the Lord in an intimate manner. St Clare shares with St Agnes in a very natural way, giving her guidance from the depths of her own relationship with God. Using inspiring words and images, she hints at ways through which St Agnes could open her heart to enter into contemplation.

As a way to open up to a dialogue with the Lord, she has this to say:

Place your mind before the mirror of eternity!
Place your soul in the brilliance of glory!
Place your heart in the figure
of the divine substance
and through contemplation
transform your entire being
into the image
of the Godhead Itself.

3 LAg 12–13

'Place your mind before the mirror of eternity': The mind is the source of all our anxieties and fears. St Clare tells us elsewhere that Christ is the mirror, so to place our mind in the mirror of eternity is to bring all that we carry within us – our burdens and our joys – to the Lord. We come before the Lord as we are and bring them to Him. Putting these things in the light of eternity has the advantage of helping us gain perspective on them. Often, our worries can diminish when we think of them in terms of eternity.

In her fourth letter to St Agnes, St Clare said, '*Gaze upon that mirror each day ... and continually study your face in it.*' This is another starting point for our prayer – to

come before the mirror, who is Christ, and ask Him, 'What are You saying to me today? What do You ask of me?' Spend some time trying to listen for His response.

'Place your soul in the brilliance of glory': The soul is our innermost being, the meeting place with God. In each of us, there is a special hidden place where God waits for us. It is in the deepest caverns of our being, where God's Word can resonate within and be amplified, if we attune ourselves to His Presence. Although not a physical place, it is where God's Spirit resides within us. In this stage, we try to imagine entering into this sacred place. We ask the Holy Spirit to illuminate it with His light. We come here in reverence, knowing it is a sacred space. We try to come in stillness and silence, so that we can be attuned to the presence of God. We may not feel anything – that is all right. The important thing is to seek to encounter Jesus.

'Place your heart in the figure of the divine substance': Let transformation take place through contemplation. Christ is the figure of the divine substance. At this stage, we seek to involve our heart. We endeavour to rest in Him, trusting in His deep love for us. We can do this by expressing sentiments of love, if we feel comfortable with that. Scripture can help us greatly here and we can

use a simple phrase, such as *'I have loved you with an everlasting love, so I am constant in my affection for you'* (Jeremiah 31) or *'Do not be afraid, for I have redeemed you ... you are mine'* (Isaiah 43). The essential point here is to do this gently. We allow ourselves to be docile in His hands, so that He can imprint Himself upon our souls.

Our aim in all of this is that we may *'feel what His friends feel'* and may *'taste the hidden sweetness'* of God. In this is true freedom of heart and where our souls may find ultimate peace.

Adoration with St Clare

Apart from Mass, the adoration of the Most Blessed Sacrament is one of the highest forms of prayer, centred as it is on Christ in the gift of Himself to us. Because He is God, He is worthy of all praise and adoration. Adoration is, above all else, an act of worship because we believe that Jesus is truly present. We look at Him with eyes of love, are moved with gratitude and we want to give Him the highest honour.

This practice of adoration is a beautiful way to prolong our encounter with Him in the celebration of Mass. When we come to adoration, we meet Jesus. It is He who has drawn us to this encounter and He longs for us to know how much He loves us. We place ourselves close to His heart, like the Beloved Disciple (John 13:25). We come to Him as we are.

There are many ways to pray at adoration – and many of the ways given in this chapter are suitable. It is good to use the time to deepen your relationship with Him – allow Him to get to know you and let Him reveal Himself to you.

St Clare is often portrayed with the Blessed Sacrament and is known for her devotion to it. Her advice was:

Gaze,
Consider,
Contemplate,
Desiring to imitate your spouse.

2 LAg 20

Breaking this down, we can see a beautiful way to pray.

Gaze upon Him: This is a powerful way to pray. St John Mary Vianney, known as The Curé of Ars who lived in the nineteenth century, spoke of a man who, when asked how he prayed, said, '*I look at Him and He looks at me.*' It is not so much a physical looking at Jesus, as putting ourselves in the presence of the One who loves us totally. We make ourselves present to Him and allow Him to look at our innermost being with His loving, healing gaze, letting the reality of His love change and heal us.

Consider Him: Having become aware of Jesus, we reflect on the reality of who He really is, as revealed to us in Scripture. Jesus came into the world to enter into

our humanity fully. No matter what way we feel, there is something in Jesus' life that each of us can relate to. For instance, if we feel fearful, we recall Jesus' fear in Gethsemane, when He prayed, '*My Father, if it is possible, let this cup pass me by*' (Matthew 26:39). If we are burdened, we hear His invitation, '*Come to me, all you who labour and are overburdened, and I will give you rest*' (Matthew 11:28–29). If we are worried about the future, we can bear in mind Jesus' words, '*I am telling you not to worry about your life and what you are to eat, nor about your body and how you are to clothe it. Look at the birds in the sky. Are you not worth much more than they are?*' (Matthew 6:25–26) Seeing afresh how Jesus works in people's lives, we can talk with Him about our life situation, and so form a relationship with Him.

For other quotations, see the 'Scripture for Reflection' section in the Further Reading and Reflections chapter.

Contemplate Him: Having spoken to the Lord about what is bothering us, we hand our cares over to Him, remembering the words of St Peter, '*Unload all your worries on to Him, since he is looking after you*' (1 Peter 5:7).

Then we rest gratefully in His loving presence, confident that He will take care of us.

As you desire to imitate Him: A fitting conclusion to a time spent in adoration with the Lord is to try to become more like Him. It is good for us to make some resolution at the end of our prayer time, even something small, like a smile, so that we enter into solidarity with Jesus.

Prayer

Jesus, send Your Spirit into my heart as
I come to You in prayer.
Give me the inner vision that St Clare had, in order to
see You as You really are.
Help me to become aware of Your
Presence with me,
especially in this time of prayer,
so that St Clare's request to 'totally love Him who gave
Himself totally for my love'
will happen in my heart.
Amen.

Praying with Scripture

Praying with Scripture is an enriching way to pray, to calm the soul. This is because using Scripture is like having a dialogue between yourself and Jesus (who is the Word of God). It contains so many comforting words from the Lord and these are like a balm to the soul.

Taking time with Scripture works on our souls in a deep way, even if we are not aware of it. Jesus compares the Word to a seed that is planted (Mark 4:26–39, Luke 8:11). We cannot see the growth and development under the soil – it is hidden, but it is happening nevertheless.

At the beginning, it can be difficult to know where to start with the Scripture. It is a good idea to start off with the gospels (where we encounter Jesus) or the Psalms (which cover the entire gamut of human emotions and which can help us to process all that is going on within us). Take a phrase from the Bible and simply ponder over it. It is good to do this each day, so that the Word becomes part of our lives. Repeating the words embeds them in our minds and hearts.

Both St Francis and St Clare had such reverence for the Word of God that they said the way of life of their brothers and sisters was to live the Holy Gospel. As we come to a deeper appreciation of the Word of God, we may be drawn to give more time to this practice and want to approach Scripture in a more structured way. *Lectio divina*, a method of praying with Scripture from the monastic tradition, helps us to do this.

Lectio Divina

This consists of four stages – *lectio, meditatio, oratio* and *contemplatio* – and is much more than a reading or study of Scripture. It is an encounter in faith and love with the Word of God. If you can devote twenty minutes or so a day to this, you will find it very helpful. And, as you reflect on these texts, do not feel that you have to exhaust one text in one day. You can come back to the texts again and again.

Lectio (**reading**): Read the text a few times. If possible, read it aloud, as there is an additional dynamic in reading it aloud. This is because the texts were meant to be proclaimed, so while you might feel self-conscious doing this, it is helpful. Several of the senses are involved (sight, speech and hearing) and it will resonate within you. This is very important in *lectio* – to allow the Word to echo and re-echo and reverberate within you. Read lingeringly, with attention and love. This is not about getting through as much text as possible, it is about allowing the Spirit who inspired the text to work on your soul, so that you may know what He wants to say to you. Savour the words, and particularly stay with words which 'speak' to you.

Meditatio (**meditation**): At this stage, mull over the text and try to see where it is being fulfilled in your life today. Your memory and imagination will enter into action as you remember past events where you have seen the Lord working or, with your imagination, enter fully into the text and become part of what is happening. Meditation takes time, but it need not stop when you finish your prayer time as you can reflect on where this is being mirrored in your life at other times – as you wait for a train, are standing in line at the shops or as you mow the lawn. Try to come to an interior understanding of what is written. Take as your example Our Lady, who '*pondered*' in her heart the things that had been revealed to her (Luke 2:19, 2:51).

Oratio (**prayer**): This is where we respond to the Lord's promptings to us in the previous stages. Taking our cue from the words of the text (usually), we base our prayer response on what has happened to us as we pondered His Word. Pray from the heart, and the Holy Spirit will put into words what we may not be able to (Romans 8:26). Even if we feel that nothing has happened, in faith make some prayer response, because the Lord is constantly working within us and His Word is dynamic.

Contemplatio (**contemplation**): Contemplation is the beginning and end of *lectio divina*. This is about entering a deeper phase in prayer. It goes beyond what our senses can experience. It is a prolonged gaze of love. From this, we are called to go forth in active love of God and our neighbour.

When you begin to pray with Scripture, it is helpful to invest in a good version of the Bible, preferably with a commentary. Throughout this book we have used the Jerusalem Bible. It is helpful to read the Bible in context, and consulting a commentary can help us to do that.

Serenity and Surrender

Being fearful and anxious can cripple us, often leaving us paralysed. Fear begins with a thought, which often latches on to other fears within us, and takes hold of us, taking us captive. The more it gets a grip, the more we can be paralysed by it. To have courage is to feel fear, but to go beyond it. One of the things that is said in Scripture most often is, '*Do not be afraid.*' When Blessed John Paul II addressed the United Nations in New York in 1979, he said:

… men and women must learn to conquer fear. We must learn not to be afraid, we must rediscover a spirit of hope and a spirit of trust. Hope is not empty optimism springing from a naïve confidence that the future will necessarily be better than the past. Hope and trust are the premise of responsible activity and are nurtured in that inner sanctuary of conscience where 'one is alone with God' and thus perceives that he or she is not alone amid the enigmas of existence, for they are surrounded by the love of the Creator.

One of the most popular prayers of our time is the 'Serenity Prayer', capturing, as it does so well, that we often struggle to deal with things that are beyond us in our daily lives.

> *God grant me the serenity to accept*
> *the things I cannot change;*
> *The courage to change the things I can;*
> *And the wisdom to know the difference.*

Reinhold Niebuhr

If we can change things that need to be dealt with, we must seek to do this with God's help. However, the pathway to serenity is to realise that we need to turn to a Higher Power when things are beyond us. We need to learn to surrender to God and let His power work in the situation.

Fr Walter Ciszek, an American Jesuit, recounted his experiences of being captured by the Russian Secret Police during the Second World War. He spent the duration of the war in Lubyanka Prison in Moscow, mostly in solitary confinement. After this, he was sent to a labour camp in Siberia for fifteen years. He was eventually exchanged for two Russian spies and returned to America, only to discover that he had been officially listed as dead for sixteen years.

During his time in Lubyanka, he underwent many interrogations because the Soviets were convinced that he was a Vatican spy. One of his greatest trials was that, having endured daily interrogations for one full year, he signed a confession that his captors had prepared. He had reached the end of his strength. Then, he was left in solitary confinement, where he was haunted by what he had done, brought down with guilt and shame. Slowly, painfully, as he struggled with the darkness that enveloped him, he realised that he had been trying all along to do everything under his own steam. He was a physically fit man, having lived a disciplined life, and possessed a sharp intellect. Each day, he had gone into the interrogations determined to outwit the men and not to give in. In fact, having struggled for so long, he reached the point of despair.

In that moment, he threw himself before the Lord and accepted his helplessness. He cried out to the Lord when he recognised, as he says himself, that his own abilities were bankrupt and God was his only hope. He was consoled in that moment by recalling the Lord in the agony in the garden, where Jesus cried out three times, *'My Father, if it be possible, let this cup pass me by'* (Matthew 26:39). He appreciated that Jesus knew the feeling of fear and weakness in His

human nature and yet He abandoned himself to the will of the Father each time.

At that moment, Fr Ciszek knew exactly what he had to do. He realised that he had to surrender himself completely to the Father and trust in Him to act in the situation, instead of trying to control it himself. He grasped that it was too big for him and that he needed power from on high. It was only when he reached the stage of being totally overwhelmed by everything that he surrendered. In doing so, he crossed a boundary that he had feared and yet, by doing this, he experienced total liberation and a release from all his fears of the future. He knew that he did not know what the future held, but he was able to trust in God to sustain him. He said:

I can only tell you frankly that my life was changed from that moment on. If my moment of despair had been a moment of total blackness, then this was an experience of blinding light. I knew immediately what I must do, what I would do, and somehow I knew that I could do it.

And this resolution carried him for what remained of his ordeal. He served another four years in Lubyanka, followed by fifteen years in Siberia. This spirituality of surrender sustained him through it all, being able to live 'one day at a time' in the same way as those who struggle with addictions.

Fr Ciszek's life is a clear witness for our times of the reality that serenity of heart comes through surrender to God. To pray in this way, to surrender, means to realise that we are helpless without God's help. We need to invite Him into the situation and hand it over to Him.

In this spirit, we offer a prayer of surrender adapted from the spiritual teachings of Fr Walter J. Ciszek SJ:

Lord, Jesus Christ, I ask the grace to accept
the sadness in my heart, as Your will for me,
in this moment. I offer it up, in union with Your
sufferings, for those who are in deepest need of
Your redeeming grace. I surrender myself to
Your Father's will and I ask You to help me
to move on to the next task that You have set for me.
Spirit of Christ, help me to enter into a
deeper union with You.

Lead me away from dwelling on the hurt I feel:
to thoughts of charity for those who need my love,
to thoughts of compassion for those
who need my care,
and to thoughts of giving to those who need my help.
As I give myself to You, help me to provide for the
salvation of those who come to me in need.
May I find my healing in this giving.
May I always accept God's will.
May I find my true self by living for
others in a spirit of sacrifice and suffering.
May I die more fully to myself, and live
more fully in You.
As I seek to surrender to the Father's will, may I come
to trust that He will do everything for me.

To surrender to God is to let ourselves be open to His action in our lives. Reaching out to others can help broaden our perspective, which, in turn, can help diminish our own pain. It is important to remember that this giving can be as simple as the gift of a smile.

Forgiveness

And when you stand in prayer, forgive whatever you have against anybody, so that your Father in heaven may forgive your failings too. But if you do not forgive, your Father in heaven will not forgive your failings either.

Mark 11:26

No book on prayer would be complete without looking at forgiveness as prayer and a way to pray. It is an absolute prerequisite. The above quotation, beginning with, '*When you stand in prayer ...*', reveals that real prayer can only flow from a heart willing to forgive. Forgiveness must be at the beginning of prayer.

The reason for this is that an absence of forgiveness is like an acid that burns away at us, eating into our very being. We feel hurt by someone, and part of us wants the person who caused the hurt to feel pain for what we perceive they have 'done' to us. However, when we dwell on it, we find ourselves replaying the situation over and over again in our heads, rehearsing what we wish we had said or done, or what we will say or do at the next opportunity! Unfortunately, we can get sucked into this;

43

sometimes it almost takes on a life of its own and it draws us deeper and deeper into itself. In the end, we cause ourselves more suffering. This is why Jesus stresses the need for forgiveness over and over again. If we don't forgive, we actually end up hurting ourselves. Each time we replay what has happened, we feel the pain again and it gets worse – it's like picking the scab off a wound; it bleeds again and can fester.

So, what is the solution?

We can't do it on our own. We require the grace of God to forgive, but we also need to co-operate with Him in this. God asks us to bless our enemies, and when we try, His grace comes to help us. Paradoxically, when we try to see the good in others, especially those who have hurt us, when we try to understand them, it diminishes the toxic quality of our anger and we start to feel calmer. As we continue to do this, we can begin to feel peace returning to our souls. It does not change the past, but it can change how we see the past and how the future will be.

It is important to realise that forgiveness is not a matter of feelings, but of the will. If we focus on our wounds, we are staying with ourselves and not focusing on God. We may not feel like forgiving someone and we may not feel

as if we like them. We are not called to 'like' people, but to love them. And so we make a decision to forgive and to let go of the injury. If necessary, we surrender it to God, so that He may take over. In its essence, forgiveness is a gift we give to ourselves.

Forgiveness has another effect too. The prayer we make on behalf of those who have hurt us also has an effect on them. We may not perceive this straight away, but it is true nonetheless. Slowly, and sometimes imperceptibly, their hearts receive healing too.

The following suggestion from Fr Silvester O'Flynn is helpful:

If you are finding it impossible to forgive somebody, it shows that you have not yet discovered the Holy Spirit within you, the Spirit given to you in Baptism. Your natural love is focusing towards that person whom you can't love. Supernatural love thinks less of towards and more of from, the source of divine love within us. Hand over this problem of forgiving to God-within-you. Confess to God that your natural ability has reached its limits. Invite God-within-you to think in your mind and to love through your heart.

All of the above will help with the day-to-day hurts that we all experience. However, sometimes an acute hurt may need deeper healing to reach the root of the pain. We may need to seek further help. The Lord often uses other people to minister to us. We may need counselling or to ask someone to pray for or with us. The suggestions given above are not a substitute for counselling when this is needed, they are given to help deal constructively with the issues that come our way each day.

The Sacrament of Reconciliation or Confession is the great source of healing and peace in difficult situations. It is a sacrament instituted by Jesus and He underscores its importance in the gospels. While it may seem very daunting to have to confess your sins to someone else, especially if you have not been to Confession in a long time, it is truly liberating, because our faith teaches us that, through the priest, it is the Lord Jesus Himself who absolves us from our sins. There is no greater freedom and joy than that experienced when you hear the words, '*I absolve you from your sins … The Lord has freed you from your sins. Go in peace.*' And this is the reality – the burden of those past sins has been taken from us and we can come to know inner peace.

As Jesus said the evening before He died, this peace is '*a peace the world cannot give*' (John 14:27).

Nevertheless, sometimes life may put us in situations that are completely unjust. We can experience hurt and we cannot understand why – there is no way to make sense of the situation, because it does not make sense. At these times, a heroic level of forgiveness may be asked of us. We need to keep our eyes and hearts firmly on Jesus and realise that this is exactly what He went through. Never was such a grave injustice done to anyone as happened to Him, and yet His prayer was: '*Father, forgive them: they do not know what they are doing*' (Luke 23:34).

While this is a difficult prayer to say when a grave injustice is being done, it goes to the depths of what our faith is about. Even if people are intentionally hurting us, they may not fully know what they are doing. To pray '*Father forgive them for they know not what they do*' is to enter into the mystery of redemption with Jesus and to trust that, in the end, His love and sacrifice will win out.

Contemplation

Contemplation is difficult to write about. As it is a wordless form of prayer, how do we find words to describe it? It is a concept-less form of prayer, so how do we find the concepts to explain it?

We are in the realm of mystery – God's mysterious way of communicating with the soul. It is because of its very intimacy that it goes beyond words. As with an embrace, words are not necessary, but very deep communication is happening nevertheless. As we are on holy ground, we have to remove the sandals of our finite ideas which seek to contain God within our own understanding (Exodus 3:5).

And yet, we should bear in mind that while contemplation is beyond concepts, it is not something that happens in a vacuum, nor are we trying to empty our minds. For St Clare and St Francis, their prayer, as with their whole lives, was centred on the person of Christ. St Clare put it beautifully when she wrote, '*totally love Him who gave Himself totally for your love*'.

Contemplation is beyond concept because Jesus Christ is not a concept, but a person, a divine person. We seek an

encounter with the One who loves us. It is a relationship that we are cultivating here, not mindlessness. Therefore, in this type of prayer, we try to put ourselves in His Presence and rest there. The prophet Hosea expressed it well when he said, *'I am going to lure her and lead her out into the wilderness and speak to her heart'* (Hosea 2:16). Blessed John Henry Newman put it more succinctly: *'Heart speaks to heart.'*

At the very heart of contemplation, we allow God to work out a transformation within us. As St Clare wrote to St Agnes of Prague:

> *Place your mind before the mirror of eternity!*
> *Place your soul in the brilliance of glory!*
> *Place your heart in the figure of*
> *the divine substance*
> *and through contemplation*
> *transform your entire being into the image*
> *of the Godhead Itself.*

St Clare captures very well what this type of prayer is about. She speaks about contemplation as bringing about the transformation of our entire being into God Himself. The words she uses make it seem as if we do this work of transformation. In fact, she is well aware

that only God can accomplish this within us. That is why she says *'through contemplation'* because contemplation is God's work within us. Earlier in the quotation, she asked St Agnes to '*place*' herself three times before the Lord – place her mind, place her soul and place her heart. It is only in our surrendering of these faculties to God that He can carry out this work. When this happens, we can co-operate with God so that this transformation can take place.

The goal of contemplation for St Clare is to allow ourselves to be open to the work of God, so that we may '*feel what His friends feel*' and '*taste the hidden sweetness*' of God.

When we start to practise this type of prayer, we find that we have all sorts of distractions. We are so used to being busy, that our minds are constantly processing things. When we try to quieten down, suddenly all the things we have to do come to mind. The really important thing is not to worry too much about this – just let those thoughts go and, as St Clare says, '*place your mind*' again before the Lord. He knows the way we operate and He just wants us to keep gently handing over everything to Him. If we imagine our prayer as a river, then these 'thoughts' are merely bits of things floating along – that's just the way it is. We don't want to grab on to them, we just see them and let them go.

It may seem strange to propose this to people with busy lives. It is true that it can take time to cultivate this type of prayer, because it is based on developing a relationship with Christ. Obviously, it is more effective if we give quality time to this. However, once you have started, it is possible to 'check in' at any time. It is like making a quick call or sending a text – it says I am still here and want to connect. The first friars had no fixed houses and so couldn't talk about 'houses of prayer', so St Francis, who was often on the move, drew on the tradition of the early monasteries and talked about entering the 'cell' of his heart. For St Francis, every friar

was in himself a 'house of prayer'. He said, '*The body is our cell; and the soul is the hermit that lives in the cell in order to pray to God and to meditate*' (*Mirror of Perfection,* 65). When he was travelling, he used to wrap his cloak about him in order to pray. For us, there are often moments when we can simply close our eyes and lift our hearts up to the Lord.

It is important to stress that this type of prayer is not about feelings. The action of God operates at a level that is deeper than the senses. We may have pleasant feelings or we may not – it doesn't matter, because this prayer is about love, real love. It requires us to be faithful. Love is a decision. We make a commitment and then take what comes. We need to be careful not to try to measure our 'success' and we should certainly never evaluate our prayer by our feelings. When you are down, don't give up.

See the 'Contemplation' section in the Further Reading and Reflections chapter for more insights.

Commitment

So far, we have reflected on the significance of prayer for our lives. It is vitally important for serenity in our souls that the way we pray is mirrored in the reality of what is happening in our lives. If these things are out of sync, then we begin to lack authenticity and may find it leads to disharmony within. Our lives should be a sign of what we believe interiorly. St Clare urges us to *'praise God by our very life'* (3 LAg 41) and so genuine prayer, which requires commitment, spills over into our lives.

Looking at how St Clare gently led her friend St Agnes, we see that the main way to have our prayer in harmony with our life is to be clearly focused on the Lord and try to stay committed to whatever we begin. There is a general fear of commitment today, but it is very true that in being dedicated, we grow and mature. St Clare herself kept before her eyes the *'one thing necessary'* (Luke 10:42), as Jesus said to Martha, and she can even say, *'I bear witness to that one thing and encourage you, for love of Him to whom you have offered yourself as a holy and pleasing sacrifice, that you always be mindful of your commitment'* (2 LAg 10).

What follows is so beautiful, we let St Clare speak to us
herself:

What you hold, may you hold.
What you do, may you do and not stop.
But with swift pace, light step, unswerving feet,
so that even your steps stir up no dust,
may you go forward
securely, joyfully and swiftly,
on the path of prudent happiness,
believing nothing,
agreeing with nothing
that would dissuade you from this commitment
or would put a stumbling block for you on the way,
so nothing prevents you from offering
your vows to the Most High in the perfection
to which the Spirit of the Lord has called you.

2 LAg 1 1 –14

Prayer

*St Clare, we ask for the grace, through your
intercession,
of being focused and single-minded.
Help us to remember how much God loves us.
May we be true to the commitments we have made
and not be afraid.
May we have courage, when this is needed,
and go forward in hope as you said,
'securely, joyfully and swiftly',
on the path of prudent happiness,
so that we may glorify God by our lives.*

Amen.

Mercy loves when love

is not deserved.

Everyday Prayers

We offer here a more traditional selection of prayers. Given our busy day-to-day lives, we are not suggesting that you take on all of them, just choose one or two that appeal to you. You could use them in the morning and evening, to begin and end the day with the Lord.

Act of Faith

You believe because you can see me.
Happy are those who have not seen and yet
* believe.*

John 20:29

Faith is vital in prayer. When Jesus performed miracles, He invariably said, '*Your faith has saved you!*' This is somewhat surprising. You might think that He would have been more impressed by people's love or their other virtues, but, no, it was faith that He responded to. In fact, when He visited Nazareth, we are told that He was unable to perform many miracles there because there was so little faith in that town. So it seems He was prevented by people's lack of faith. It is a necessary prerequisite. Perhaps this is because, if we demonstrate faith, it shows that we trust God and this removes any barriers that may be in our hearts. As St Mark tells us, '*Everything is possible for anyone who has faith*' (9:23).

An 'Act of Faith' is not so much a prayer for faith, as an assertion of our belief. In saying this prayer, we give due honour to God and also put our faith into practice. This very exercise helps to deepen and strengthen our faith.

Act of Faith

My God,

I believe in You and in

all Your Church teaches,

because You have said it

and Your Word is true.

Act of Hope

The 'Act of Hope' articulates that our hope is fuelled by our belief. We believe the promises of Christ, because He is God and speaks the truth. Hope is also strengthened by confidence in His infinite power.

Perhaps it is nourished most of all by our trust in God's mercy. Mercy loves when love is not deserved. If we were to get what we truly deserve, we would have no hope. But we need have no fear of Him or the future.

It might seem that faith and love are more important. But actually it is hope that bolsters up our faith and our love. In the nineteenth century, Charles Péguy wrote a poem in which there were three sisters who had joined hands – Faith and Love are the big sisters with the little girl, Hope, in the middle. Looking on, it seemed that Faith and Hope were helping the little girl but, as they got nearer, it was Hope, running ahead, who brought her sisters along. Hope reminds us that we are reaching towards a greater goal than the more immediate ones. It urges us to keep going.

Our 'Act of Hope' is not so much a prayer for hope, as an articulation of the hope we have, trusting that in exercising this hope, it will grow.

Act of Hope

My God

I hope in You for grace

and glory,

because of your promises, Your mercy

and Your power.

Act of Love

Nothing therefore can come between us and the love of Christ, even if we are troubled or worried, or being persecuted, or lacking food or clothes, or being threatened or even attacked.

Romans 8:31, 35

Jesus said the greatest commandment was to love '*The Lord God with your whole heart*' (Mark 12:29). He continued, '*You must love your neighbour as yourself*' Marke 12:31). However, love is not about how we feel. We make the decision to love and then carry through with it. We may feel that we don't love God with our whole heart. Still, we must aspire to it and keep the ideal before our eyes, to inspire us to keep trying. God deserves our best.

Our 'Act of Love' reinforces these sentiments in our hearts and helps to strengthen our resolve to love. It also quite clearly states that we cannot do this without God's grace.

From the depths of your heart love God.

St Clare

Act of Love

My God,

because You are so good,

I love You with my whole heart,

and for Your sake,

I love my neighbour as myself.

Act of Contrition

Give me again the joy of Your help,
With a spirit of fervour sustain me.

Psalm 50

One of Jesus' most popular stories is the parable of the Prodigal Son (Luke 15). It reveals the true picture of the Heavenly Father, who watches out for His children, running out to meet them. We also see His young son, rehearsing his lines – '*Father, I have sinned against heaven and against you.*' However, the Father, who is slow to anger and rich in mercy, does not let him finish his speech, but runs out to embrace him and reinstates him with his dignity as His son. Similarly, we often reject the loving advances God makes towards us, even in spite of ourselves.

In Psalm 50, which is said to have been composed by King David after he had committed adultery and murder, we see how liberating repentance is. King David realised the enormity of what he had done and turned to the Lord, trusting that he will not be rejected.

In praying our 'Act of Contrition', we repent of the hurt caused by our betrayals, both of God and of our brothers

and sisters. We ask for His grace, so that we may be strengthened interiorly and be energised to make a new beginning, a fresh start.

Act of Contrition

My God, I am very sorry

I have sinned against You,

Because You are so good,

and with the help of

Your grace I will not

sin again.

Our Father

The 'Our Father' holds pride of place among all other prayers. It is what Jesus taught the disciples when they said to Him, *'Lord, teach us to pray'* (Luke 11:1). Therefore, it is a precious gift from Our Saviour to us and we should treasure it as such.

A good way to pray the 'Our Father' is to imagine Jesus is standing beside you, perhaps holding your hand, or with His arm around you. The fact that the prayer starts off with 'Our Father' and not 'My Father' is an indication that we are not alone when we pray this prayer.

It is through what Jesus accomplished for us that we have been adopted as children of the Father and, in this prayer, we can go to the Father, accompanied by Jesus. If we fully realised what a privilege this is, to call God (the creator of the universe) our 'father', we would spend our whole lives giving thanks for it. In fact, when St Francis used to pray the 'Our Father', he was so overwhelmed by this fact that he often got no further than the words 'Our Father' and stayed with those words in love and adoration.

Our Father

Our Father who art in heaven,

hallowed be Thy Name.

Thy kingdom come.

Thy will be done on earth, as it is in heaven.

Give us this day our daily bread,

and forgive us our trespasses,

as we forgive those who trespass against us,

and lead us not into temptation,

but deliver us from evil.

Novena to the Sacred Heart

(M)any of us in years gone by will remember seeing a picture or statue of the Sacred Heart. It was usually given a prominent place in most Irish homes and was often accompanied by a little red lamp.

The origins of this devotion go back to the thirteenth century and our own St Bonaventure. In following the footsteps of St Francis, St Bonaventure desired to reveal to people the beauty of the Incarnation of Our Lord, and what better way than to speak of the love in the Heart of Jesus for each one of us.

Four centuries later, Our Lord appeared to St Margaret Mary Alacoque in France. When resting her head on His chest, she experienced the beating in His breast. He asked her to spread this devotion and attached twelve promises to those who prayed to His Sacred Heart. June is the month of the Sacred Heart.

The most recognisable phrase associated with this devotion is: '*Sacred Heart of Jesus I place all my trust in You.*'

Novena to the Sacred Heart

You have said, O Divine Jesus,

'Ask and you shall receive, Seek and you shall find,

Knock and the door shall be opened unto you.'

Relying on these promises, I come with confidence

during this novena to beg of you the favours I need

(make your request here)

From whom shall I ask, Lord Jesus, if not from You,

whose heart is an unfailing source of grace.

Most loving heart of my God,

I believe in Your power,

I believe in Your knowledge,

I believe in Your personal love for me.

And therefore, O Sacred Heart of Jesus,

I place all my trust in You.

ɲail ʍarƴ

In her third letter, St Clare says, '*Cling to His Most Sweet Mother.*' For St Clare, Our Lady is always mentioned in relation to Jesus. He is always the focus of her attention but, being a woman deeply in love, she understands the depth of the love that exists between them – and, being the 'mother' of at least fifty sisters in her monastery, she knew what was involved in this role. A mother always has time for all her children and has all their interests at heart. She unifies the family, is a refuge when we are afraid, the one we can always turn to, no matter how much we think others may not love us or, indeed, how much we may not love ourselves! Jesus gave His mother to us as our mother in a special way on the Cross, and so St Clare knew that we can all approach Our Lady in complete confidence, knowing that we will not be turned away.

When we pray to Our Lady, we seek to develop a relationship with her. We take time to talk to her and share our worries and joys with her. We confide in her, let her become a true mother to us. If we '*cling*' to her, as St Clare suggests, she won't let us down.

ɦail ᙢarʏ

Hail Mary,

Full of grace,

The Lord is with thee.

Blessed art thou amongst women

And blessed is the fruit of thy womb,

Jesus.

Holy Mary, mother of God,

Pray for us now and at the hour of our death.

Amen.

On Prayer to Our Lady

Look to the star – call upon Mary!

In danger, in difficulty or in doubt,

think of Mary, call upon Mary,

keep her name on your lips,

never let it pass out of your heart.

Following her footsteps,

you will not go astray;

praying to her,

you will not fall into despair;

thinking of her you will not err.

While she keeps hold of your hand,

you will not fall,

you will not grow weary,

you will have no fear.

Enjoying her protection,

you will reach the goal.

Mary, Star of the Sea, pray for us.

St Bernard

Memorare

Remember O most gracious virgin Mary,

that never was it known

that anyone who fled to your protection,

implored your help or sought your intercession

was left unaided.

Inspired with this confidence, I fly unto you,

O Virgin of virgins, my mother;

to you do I come, before you I stand,

sinful and sorrowful;

O Mother of the Word Incarnate,

despise not my petition,

but in thy mercy hear and answer me.

Amen.

The Rosary

If the 'Our Father' is Jesus' gift to us, then most certainly the Rosary is Our Lady's gift to us, her children. It is a beautiful prayer that concentrates on meditating upon the mysteries of the life of Jesus in the company of Mary. It is an entirely scriptural prayer, the simplicity of which is deceptive, as it hides profound depths of meaning.

It is also a prayer that is particularly suitable for people with busy lives. It lends itself to being prayed 'on the go'. The rhythmic repetition of the prayers has a calming effect on us. It is not so much concentrating on the words that is the key, as an awareness that we are not alone while we are praying – the words serve to uphold us, as we reflect on the mysteries.

In a world where the value of silence is little appreciated, praying the Rosary together gives a 'window' of opportunity for silence, when the family is together. Our lives are so busy that it may not happen at any other time. A family that tries to do this can carve out a quarter of an hour in the day where there is silence, which creates a deep bond in the Spirit, even without there being any awareness that this is happening. It may not seem that it

actually is a silent time, but these moments spent praying with Our Lady subtly deepen the unity of the family.

How to Pray the Rosary

The Rosary is a prayer that meditates on the mysteries of Christ's life. The complete Rosary consists of four sets of mysteries – the Joyful Mysteries, the Sorrowful Mysteries, the Mysteries of Light and the Glorious Mysteries – each prayed on different days of the week.

To begin the Rosary, you pray the Apostles' Creed on the crucifix of the rosary beads. After this, you pray the 'Our Father', three 'Hail Marys' and a 'Glory be to the Father' on the beads connecting the crucifix to the circle of beads.

Then, you come to the mysteries (otherwise known as 'decades' because they each contain ten 'Hail Marys'). Begin by announcing the title of the mystery. For each mystery, you pray one 'Our Father', ten 'Hail Marys' and one 'Glory be to the Father'. After this, you may pray the 'Fatima Prayer'. Then, you announce the next mystery and pray it in the same way, and so on.

When you have completed the five mysteries, add one 'Our Father', one 'Hail Mary' and one 'Glory be to the Father' for the pope's intentions. Then you may say the 'Hail, Holy Queen' prayer.

The Joyful Mysteries

Prayed on Monday and Saturday

The Annunciation
The Visitation
The Birth of Our Lord
The Presentation in the Temple
The Finding of the Child Jesus in the Temple

The Sorrowful Mysteries

Prayed on Tuesday and Friday

The Agony in the Garden
The Scourging at the Pillar
The Crowning with Thorns.
The Carrying of the Cross
The Crucifixion

The Mysteries of Light

Prayed on Thursday

The Baptism of Jesus
The Wedding Feast of Cana
The Proclamation of the Kingdom
The Transfiguration
The Institution of the Eucharist

The Glorious Mysteries

Prayed on Wednesday and Sunday

The Resurrection
The Ascension
The Descent of the Holy Spirit on
the Apostles and Our Lady
The Assumption
The Crowning of Our Lady as the
Queen of Heaven

The Prayers of the Rosary

The Apostles' Creed

Fatima Prayer

Hail, Holy Queen

The Apostles' Creed

I believe in God,
the Father Almighty
Creator of heaven and earth.
And in Jesus Christ,
His only Son, Our Lord
Who was conceived by the Holy Spirit,
born of the Virgin Mary,
suffered under Pontius Pilate,
was crucified, died and was buried;
He descended into hell;
on the third day He rose again from the dead;
He ascended into heaven,
and is seated at the right hand
of God the Father Almighty;
from there He will come to judge
the living and the dead.
I believe in the Holy Spirit,
the holy Catholic Church,
the communion of saints,
the forgiveness of sins,
the resurrection of the body,
and life everlasting.
Amen.

Fatima Prayer

O my Jesus, forgive us our sins,

save us from the fires of hell;

lead all souls to heaven,

especially those in most need of your mercy.

Hail, Holy Queen

Hail, Holy Queen, mother of mercy; hail, our life, our sweetness and our hope! To you do we cry, poor banished children of Eve; to you do we send up our sighs, mourning and weeping in this valley of tears. Turn then, most gracious advocate, your eyes of mercy towards us; and after this our exile, show unto us the blessed fruit of your womb, Jesus.
O clement, O loving, O sweet Virgin Mary.

V. Pray for us, O Holy Mother of God.
R. That we may be made worthy of the promises of Christ.

Let us pray.
O God, whose only-begotten Son, by his life, death and resurrection, has purchased for us the rewards of eternal life; grant we beseech you, that meditating on these Mysteries of the most holy rosary of the Blessed Virgin Mary, we may both imitate what they contain, and obtain what they promise, through the same Christ our Lord.

R. Amen.

The Angelus

This prayer is a wonderful way to bring our hearts and minds to the Lord during the day. It is traditional to pray it at 6 a.m., 12 noon and 6 p.m. – literally at morning, noon and night! It has the effect of sanctifying our day as we begin it (at daybreak), during the course of the day (by pausing to pray at midday) and by ending our day in thanksgiving at 6 p.m., which equates to sundown. 'The Angelus' focuses on the mystery of the incarnation of the Lord and reaches its climax with the breathtaking proclamation of St John, '*The Word became flesh and dwelt among us.*'

When we pray this prayer, we pray that the implications of Jesus becoming one with us, in order to save us, may be fully realised in our lives. In 'The Angelus', Our Lady is held up to us as a model, for her prompt and whole-hearted response to the Lord, '*Let what you have said be done to me*' (Luke 1:38). We ask that her prayers help us to respond as she did. We pray that the Lord will pour forth His grace into our hearts, so that by the power of His passion, we may be brought to the glory of His resurrection.

Praying 'The Angelus' is also an opportunity for us to be more 'bold' about our faith: stopping for a few minutes for this prayer is a simple but powerful witness to our belief.

The Angelus

V. **The Angel of the Lord declared unto Mary.**

R. *And she conceived of the Holy Spirit.*

The 'Hail Mary'

V. **Behold the handmaid of the Lord.**

R. *Be it done unto me according to Your Word.*

The 'Hail Mary'

V. **And the Word was made flesh.**

R. *And dwelt among us.*

The 'Hail Mary'

V. **Pray for us, O Holy Mother of God.**

R. *That we may be made worthy of the promises of Christ.*

Let us pray. Pour forth, we beseech You, O Lord, Your grace into our hearts, that we to whom the Incarnation of Christ, Your Son, was made known by the message of an angel, may by His passion and cross be brought to the glory of His resurrection, through the same Christ Our Lord. Amen.

May the divine assistance remain always with us and may the souls of the faithful departed, through the mercy of God, rest in peace. Amen.

Then say the 'Glory Be to the Father' three times.

Praying to St Joseph

The basic facts about St Joseph are well known. He was chosen by God to be the spouse of Mary. In the scriptures, he is revealed as a strong yet gentle man. His only moment of hesitation in carrying out the divine mission presented to him was when he considered breaking his espousal with Mary after she told him she was pregnant.

He was a man of tremendous courage and initiative shown when he travelled to Egypt to protect the little baby Jesus from Herod's soldiers who slaughtered all babies around Bethlehem, thus ensuring that this child, the promised King of Israel, would be spared.

At Knock Shrine in County Mayo, Ireland, St Joseph appeared together with Our Lady and St John, the only time he is known to have appeared to anyone. He came as a tall, silent and protective figure, casting his gaze towards Our Lady and Jesus, who came as the Lamb of God. He reveals himself as truly humble, someone who is powerful with God – though how could he be otherwise: he was chosen by God to be the earthly father of His Son, Jesus.

His principal feast day is celebrated on 19 March but he is also honoured as patron saint of workers and that feast day is held on 1 May. St Joseph is also the patron saint of the universal church and the dying.

Prayer to St Joseph

O glorious St Joseph,

You who have power to render possible

things that are for us impossible,

come to our aid in our present

trouble and distress.

Take this important and difficult

affair under your particular

protection,

that it may end happily.

O dear St Joseph, all our confidence

is in you since you are so powerful

with Jesus and Mary.

Let it not be said that we would

invoke you in vain.

Amen.

Why Do People Pray to the Saints?

In Baptism, a child is given a name, preferably a saint's name. Later, in their school years, the child chooses a name at Confirmation, again a saint's name is recommended. This is someone the child can look up to, model their lives on and get to know through reading about them. The saints are those who remained faithful to Christ's teaching and left us an example of a way to follow.

Their holiness was confirmed when the Church pronounced them saints.

St Clare followed the monastic way. She had great devotion to Christ in the Blessed Sacrament. Her prayer of intercession brought comfort and healing to many. In tune with the Spirit, she had that inner strength and conviction that radiated to all who sought her out.

Prayer to St Clare

Blessed St Clare,

You trusted in the Blessed Sacrament

as your only protection.

In your hour of need you heard a

voice from the Sacred Host:

'I will always take care of you.'

We entrust our needs to you, especially

(here mention requests)

Enkindle in us a tender love for Jesus and Mary.

Help us to trust Him as you did.

Intercede for our families, our friends,

our youth and all those who need our prayers.

We pray for our church, our country

and our suffering world.

Amen.

Prayer to my Guardian Angel

O Angel of God my guardian dear,

To whom God's love commits me here,

Ever this day (night) be at my side,

To light and guard, to rule and guide.

Amen.

Morning Offering

Almighty Lord God,

You have brought us to the beginning of another day.

Strengthen us with Your grace,

so that during this day we may not fall into any sin,

but may direct all our thoughts, words and actions,

to accomplish Your Holy Will.

Through Christ our Lord.

Amen

Prayer at Night

Jesus, Mary and Joseph, I give you my

heart and my soul,

Jesus, Mary and Joseph, assist me now and

in my last agony,

Jesus, Mary and Joseph, may I breathe forth

my soul in peace with you.

Amen.

Into Your Hands

Into Your hands

Lord, I commend my Spirit.

Lord Jesus, receive my soul.

Amen.

Daily Prayer for Protection

In the name of Jesus,

I put my conscious mind, my unconscious mind

my subconscious mind, my thoughts, my memory

my emotions and my words

under the protection of the Precious Blood of Jesus.

Establish Your Lordship there

and keep me as Your own.

Amen

For the Whole Human Family

Keep watch, dear Lord, with those who work,

or watch, or weep this night,

and give Your angels charge over those who sleep.

Tend the sick, Lord Christ, give rest to the weary,

bless the dying, soothe the suffering,

pity the afflicted, shield the joyous,

and all for Your love's sake.

Amen.

Prayer Before the Crucifix

This prayer was written by St Francis:

Most High,

glorious God,

enlighten the darkness of my heart

and give me

true faith,

certain hope

and perfect charity,

sense and knowledge,

Lord,

that I may carry out

Your holy and true command.

Prayer for Peace

Though not written by him, this prayer is attributed to St Francis, as it reflects the dispositions of his heart.

Lord, make me an instrument of your peace,

Where there is hatred, let me sow love;

Where there is injury, pardon;

Where there is doubt, faith;

Where there is despair, hope;

Where there is darkness, light;

And where there is sadness, joy,

O Divine Master,

grant that I may not so much seek

to be consoled, as to console;

to be understood as to understand;

to be loved as to love.

For it is in giving that we receive;

It is in pardoning that we are pardoned;

and it is in dying that we are born to eternal life.

Prayer for the Faithful Departed

Eternal rest grant unto them, O Lord,

and let perpetual light shine on them.

May they rest in peace.

Amen.

Prayers and
Reflections
for Our Times

In this age of hi-tech gadgets and cyberspace, what relevance could a medieval saint possibly have for us? It is eight hundred years since St Clare left home and began the Poor Clare Order along with St Francis. The following reflections and prayers are an attempt to introduce this extraordinary woman to the people of our times, and to look at ways in which she can continue to inspire us today.

In Times of Insecurity and Anxiety

In this time of great change, when so many things we took for granted are no longer certain, the world seems to be out of control, we can marvel at how St Clare trusted that Jesus would always come through for her – He Himself was the Way, when it was unclear what would happen next. In response to a friar who was encouraging her to be patient during her final illness, she replied in a firm voice:

After I once came to know the grace of my Lord Jesus Christ through his servant Francis, no pain has been bothersome, no penance too severe, no weakness, dearly beloved brother, has been hard.

What is striking is her courage, right to the end.

She lived trusting that '*by turning everything to their good God co-operates with all those who love him*' (Romans 8:28). In this spirit we pray.

In Times of Insecurity and Anxiety

Lord Jesus,

in these insecure, anxious times,

we are stretched

in so many ways,

spiritually,

physically,

financially.

People are no longer given

their true dignity,

and so much that we treasure is gone.

It is hard at times to trust.

Help us to anchor ourselves in You,

whose love for us is unchanging.

May Your Spirit lead us in Your way.

May Your hope give us

the peace of soul You promise.

Amen.

Pray for Guidance in Difficult Times

At the beginnings of St Clare's new religious community, the sisters had to contend with many difficulties. St Clare goes as far as outlining some of them in her rule – '*poverty, hard work, trial, shame or the contempt of the world*'.

When St Francis saw how well the sisters had coped with all their difficulties, he was very moved and he gave them a Form of Life, which was to be their guiding inspiration. In it he said they had '*… taken the Holy Spirit as a spouse*', and it is clear from her life that St Clare had. This is an unusual term for a nun, as Blessed John Paul II said, but he also said that it showed that there was a 'resonance' between her life and Luke's account of the Annunciation, when Our Lady was filled with the Holy Spirit.

The Holy Spirit strengthened Our Lady to deal with suffering in her life. And the Holy Spirit was the source of St Clare's inner strength too.

As she lay dying, St Clare spoke these words to her soul:

The One who created you has infused the Holy Spirit in you and then guarded you as a mother does her littlest child.

PC 11:3

St Clare lived her life in the light of the Holy Spirit's grace and this sustained her in all her difficulties and carried her at this final hurdle. In this spirit, we pray a prayer written by St Francis (Lt Ord 50–52).

Prayer for Guidance in Difficult Times

Almighty, eternal, just and merciful God,

Give us miserable ones

the grace to do for You alone

what we know You want us to do

and always to desire what pleases You.

Inwardly cleansed,

interiorly enlightened

and inflamed by the fire of the Holy Spirit,

may we be able to follow

in the footprints of Your beloved Son,

our Lord Jesus Christ,

and, by Your grace alone,

may we make our way to You,

Most High,

Who live and rule

in perfect Trinity and simple Unity,

and are glorified

God almighty,

forever and ever.

Amen.

When Our Fears Overwhelm Us

We will all experience times when the fear within seems to engulf us. When this happens, it seems that we cannot see the way forward. We are often paralysed by these fears and anxieties. It is part of the human condition. Perhaps that is why one of the things we hear most in Scripture is '*Do not be afraid*' (Isaiah 43:1) or '*Do not let your hearts be troubled*' (John 14:1). It seems that God knows that we need to have it hammered home to us. He is stronger than our fears and He has conquered. We need only entrust ourselves to Him and we can claim His strength, which comes from the Holy Spirit.

St Clare had very little material security in her life. She faced huge obstacles bravely, trusting in God. In writing to her friend St Agnes of Prague and seeking to encourage her in the difficulties she was experiencing, she said (2 LAg 13–14):

Go forward
securely, joyfully and swiftly,
on the path of prudent happiness
believing nothing, agreeing with nothing
that would dissuade you from this commitment.
In this spirit we pray.

When Our Fears Overwhelm Us

Lord,

I am often filled with fear when I think of the future.

I am haunted by past mistakes and hurts,

afraid of what the future might hold

and I feel paralysed.

I surrender it all to You now.

I ask You to heal all that is wounded in me

and trust You to take care of all I worry about.

You are the One

who makes all things new.

With You I will go forward,

securely and joyfully,

into freedom.

Amen.

For Our Sense of Self-Esteem, Dignity and Worth

Today, self-fulfilment is of concern to many people – and, of course, it is important to develop ourselves to our full potential. However, if our focus is concentrated on ourselves, we will never find contentment, because a life that is self-centred is not a happy one. What is important is to try and find the balance between realising that everything we have received is a gift and, then, having the liberty to relax into enjoying this with a grateful heart, because Jesus came that we may have life to the full (John 10).

When St Clare was called by the Lord, she deliberately set out on a path that was uncertain, living a life of poverty that left her exposed and vulnerable. In this, she learned to depend on God to carry her. As she grew into this way of life and saw that the Lord actually did support her, she came to appreciate more and more how much she was loved. And it was this that nurtured her true self-worth, and gave her an inner strength that continued to grow. When the time came for her to die, she cried out, '*May You be blessed, O Lord, You who have created my soul*' (L Cl 46). It is very beautiful to think that at the end of her life, she had no regrets and was happy to be who she was. It shows a great inner strength and harmony. And so we pray.

For Our Sense of Self-Esteem, Dignity and Worth

Lord,

You tell us in Scripture that we are precious in Your

eyes and that You love us (Isaiah 43:4).

Help us to truly believe this, so that we can come to

appreciate our true worth.

We seek happiness in many ways,

chasing the latest products,

thinking they will make us more acceptable.

And yet our hearts are created for greater things and

remain restless until they rest in You.

We ask You to heal the wounded areas of our hearts.

Help us to make a gift of ourselves to others,

so that we may find ourselves in this giving.

Let us come to appreciate our giftedness, so that we

can come to thank You for creating us.

Amen.

III

On the Grace of Work when Employed

St Clare was determined that the sisters would not earn revenue from property. Instead, she wanted the sisters to rely on the providence of God, keeping themselves by the work of their hands. She spoke of '*the grace of work*', for she realised that to be able to work was, in itself, a great gift. When we can do something productive, it gives meaning to our lives.

The reality of life in their monastery was very difficult, with about fifty sisters living in a very cramped space, with no fixed income. What prevented this from disheartening them and reducing their existence to mere drudgery was the attitude that St Clare inspired in them. She stressed that they were to be employed in such a way that '*idleness, which is the enemy of the soul*' is banished and which would not extinguish the '*spirit of prayer and devotion*'. For her, as for St Francis, this '*spirit of prayer and devotion*' was the most important thing and everything else had to take a back seat. She saw their work as enabling them to return to the Lord an increase in the talents given by Him and so kept the Lord's goodness to them before their eyes constantly, as their incentive.

On the Grace of Work when Employed

Lord, we thank You for the gifts You have given us.

We thank You especially for the grace of employment.

We thank You for the work that we do

and the people we work with.

We ask You to help us as we work,

so that we may apply ourselves to

the best of our ability.

When we struggle or feel stressed out,

or are just bogged down with the drudgery of it all,

help us to have a clear vision of purpose in our lives.

We pray for those who are unhappy in their work,

especially those who experience bullying.

May Your grace help and sustain them.

Amen.

The Grace of Work and Dealing with Unemployment

So many people cannot work, either because they cannot find work (which is a very big issue today) or because they are unable to work. St Clare appreciated that our dignity does not depend on what we do; it is the quality of our lives that matters. Every human being has an inherent dignity because we are made in the image and likeness of God. In this, she is a great witness to us today, when unemployment is so high. She knew the interior struggle of being unable to work because she was invalided for the last twenty-seven years of her life. This brought her into dependence on

others, so she can empathise with us in our daily struggles.

St Clare outlined some of the difficulties that the community in San Damiano, which had about fifty sisters in it, had to struggle with – '*deprivation, poverty, hard work, trial, shame or the contempt of the world*'. As their leader, she was intensely aware of what was needed to provide for them all.

And, in the midst of all of that, she fell ill and remained bedridden for the remainder of her life. It is clear that, though not unemployed in the sense that we would look at it today, she experienced many of the things that those who are unemployed have to contend with – insecurity, the sense of not being able to contribute in the way that we would like to, not being able to exercise our abilities. In addition, there are the things she mentions herself – poverty, deprivation and shame.

Yet somehow, living in such dependence, she came to a serene acceptance of what was her lot. She saw that Christ was most powerful and accomplished the most when everything was stripped of Him on the Cross. She gained inspiration from that.

The Grace of Work and Dealing with Unemployment

Heavenly Father,

We thank You for the gifts that You have given us.

We thank You also for our present condition, of not

being able to work.

It is hard to thank You for that, but even so we believe

that Your Will for our lives

is where we will find most fulfilment.

And so we ask You for the graces we need at this time,

to cope with it all, because it is very difficult.

We ask You to provide for our needs.

Help us when the insecurity and fears rob us of peace.

Help us also when we feel intimidated and our dignity

is threatened.

Let us find employment in which we will find fulfilment

and contribute in a positive way to society.

We ask this in Jesus' name.

Amen.

St Clare and Healing the Sick

St Clare was a saint who knew the reality of sickness at first hand – she was bed-ridden (more or less) for the last twenty-seven years of her life. According to the testimonies of her sisters, she bore her infirmity well and was a source of consolation and refuge for all of them. Not only that, the sisters came to her when they were finding it too difficult to cope with their own illnesses. Many of them testified that they were cured by her prayers.

St Francis also turned to her when healing was needed. He sent friars in need of healing to her for prayer and, when very ill himself, he came to San Damiano, the monastery of St Clare, in order to be taken care of.

At this time, when he was extremely sick, he wrote a canticle for the sisters in which he said, '*Those weighed down by sickness and the others wearied because of them, all of you: bear it in peace*' (Ct Exh 5).

Her own experience of illness enabled St Clare to respond with compassion for those suffering. And yet she encouraged them to see beyond the present pain. She wrote:

If you suffer with Him, you will reign with Him,
weeping with Him, you will rejoice with Him.

2 LAg 21

Confident of having someone who knows what the pain
of sickness involves, we ask her to pray for us now.

Prayer to
St Clare in Sickness

St Clare, lover of the poor Christ,

Who bore your own sufferings with patience,

whose trust in God's promises

helped you to keep going in your own suffering.

You lovingly tended the sick in your own monastery:

you were there for anyone who asked your help,

and interceded for them in their misery.

We ask you to intercede for us with Jesus,

who always heeded your prayers

and obtain for us the healing of which

we are in such need.

Amen.

Prayers for Special Intentions

At different times in our lives we have special intentions that are close to our heart. Sometimes, we are not able to put these intentions into words. At such times, it is consoling to read in scripture: *'The Spirit too comes to help us in our weakness, so when we cannot choose words in order to pray properly, the Spirit Himself expresses our plea in a way that could never be put into words'* (Romans 8:26). However, it is often helpful to be able to express these needs. We are asked to pray for many of these intentions and we offer the following prayers to try to articulate some of them.

A Parent's Prayer

Dear Lord,

I thank you for the gift of my children. I thank You for the gift of faith that you have given me. I ask You to keep me faithful and to give me the grace to pass this on to them, so that they grow up loving You and knowing that they are loved by You.

Keep them safe. I worry so much about them sometimes, because the world in which we live today has so many dangers. I cannot possibly watch over them constantly, and so I ask you to do this. Give them good friends who will help them mature and develop into caring adults.

I thank You for their health and I ask You to give them continued good health. I know that they are precious in Your sight. I know that You love them even more than I do and so I entrust them to Your care. I consecrate myself and all my family to Your divine mercy.

Amen.

Let the little children come to me,

and do not stop them.

Luke 18:16

Prayer for Those Unable to Sleep

Lord,

Please help me to sleep tonight. I find it so hard when I cannot sleep. The more I think about it, the more restless and anxious I get. It defeats the purpose, I know, but I can't seem to help it. I should go to bed because I need the sleep, but part of me dreads the long hours of darkness.

Let Your Holy Spirit fill me with Your peace, so that I can relax and get the sleep I need. And, if I cannot sleep, give me the deep serenity in my heart of knowing that I am loved by You and that You want me to rest in Your love.

Amen.

Unload all your worries on to Him,

since He is looking after you.

1 Peter 5:7

Prayer for Healing at Bedtime

Heavenly Father,

I thank You that You always take care of me.

Fill me with Your Holy Spirit.

There are so many areas where I need healing

(Pause for a moment to think of the areas that come to mind; particularly recall incidents that have occurred during the day)

Holy Spirit, let Your grace repair those areas now.

Heal the wounds I am not aware of,

especially things that are an obstacle to love of God and my neighbour.

Prayer for healing at bedtime

Heavenly Father,

I repent of any ways that I have offended You, consciously or unconsciously.

As I settle down to sleep, I surrender it all to You.

I ask for the gift of a good night's sleep.

I trust that Your healing action will continue through the night because,

'He pours gifts on His beloved while they slumber.'
  (Psalm 126)

I entrust myself and my family to Your mercy.

I ask all of this in Jesus' name.

Amen.

Prayer for a Parent with a Sick Child

Dear Lord,

I thank You for the precious gift of my child. I ask You to heal them. You know how much it upsets me to see them suffer. I feel so helpless, unable to take their pain away and I can do so little to help them. I beg You to bring relief to them. You are our loving Father and I believe that You therefore understand exactly how I feel.

Please help me to be what I should be in this situation and give me the grace to trust in You always. I believe that in Your will is our peace, but please help me to live this out, as I find it so hard when they are suffering. I entrust them to Your care. I ask this in Jesus' name.

Amen.

Jesus said, 'Do not be afraid; only have faith.' Taking with Him the child's father and mother and His own companions, He went into the place where the child lay. And taking the child by the hand, He said to her, 'Talitha, kum' which means, 'Little girl, I tell you to get up.'

Mark 36:40-41

Prayer for a Person Suffering from Illness

Dear Lord,

I ask You to heal me. I feel so wretched and it seems to be constant. When I am submerged by sickness, it takes over and I can think of nothing else. I ask You to lay Your healing hands on me and bring me some relief. I believe in Your power to heal, which You showed so much when You were on earth. I believe that You want only what is best for me, and so I ask You to give me the graces I need.

If it is not Your will that I be healed at this time, please support me through this struggle. Send Your Holy Spirit to comfort and strengthen me. I ask You especially to bless those who are looking after me. I trust in You and Your great love for me, and so I leave myself in Your hands.

Amen.

Lord, heal me, my body is racked:

my soul is racked with pain.

Psalm 6:2–3

For Those who Feel Lonely, Abandoned or Rejected

Dear Lord,

Sometimes I feel so lonely and seem to get engulfed by these feelings. The more I think about it, the more I get bogged down by it all. Let me experience Your deep love for me, so that I may be strengthened in my inner self. Let me find my security in You, so that, even when I am alone, I may not feel this dreadful loneliness.

I know that if this sense of being loved by You takes a deep root in my heart, that my self-worth will return and that I will find it easier to have the confidence to face situations in life that I often avoid now and which leave me feeling lonely. I ask you to heal me of this. I trust in You – let me not be disappointed.

Amen.

You are precious in my eyes

and I love you.

Isaiah 43:4

Prayer for People with Suicidal Thoughts

Lord,

I beg You to help me with Your grace. I feel so desperate and am so burdened at this time that I can see no way out of the rut I am in. My whole life seems to be crumbling around me and I feel that I cannot go on. I know deep down that You have created all life and that it is sacred, but it feels like life is no longer worth living. I know, too, that You have created me and love me. I know also that You came that we may have life and have it to the full.

Please help me to experience that, as I seem to be struggling to exist at the moment. I beg You to allow Your love for me to penetrate the darkness that I am living in, because I know that it has the power to change me. Let Your Holy Spirit fill me with hope for the future and give me the security that I crave. I entrust myself to Your divine mercy.

Amen.

As soon as Peter felt the force of the wind,

he took fright and began to sink.

'Lord! Save me!'

Jesus put His hand out at once

and held him.

Matthew 14:30–31

Prayer for Those
Bereaved through Suicide

Lord,

I ask You to have mercy on _____ who has taken his / her life and on all those who have taken their life. You alone know what burdens they were carrying. I ask You to forgive anything that needs to be forgiven and to let them enjoy eternal happiness with You. I ask You to give us the graces we need at this time as we struggle to come to terms with our loss. Nothing we have ever lived through could have prepared us for this.

Even as we try to cope with this loss, help us to overcome the deep, gnawing sense of guilt that we feel – even though we know that this feeling, that maybe there was something more we could have done, is senseless. I ask You to heal and strengthen us and bring us through these difficult times. I find great comfort in knowing that You are the Good Shepherd and that, even as we go through this dark valley, we do not need to be afraid, because You are with us and will comfort us (Psalm 22).

Amen.

He will wipe away all tears from their eyes; there will be no more death, and no more mourning or sadness, because the former things have passed away.

Revelation 21:4

Prayer for Those Suffering with Depression

Lord,

You know the darkness that envelops me. This cloud descends on me and, when it does, I seem to lose all perspective. It seems like it will never lift. I know I have pulled out of it before, but when it starts again, it clouds everything. Help me to trust in You in this difficult time. I know that after the rain, the sun shines again and that above the clouds, the sun is always shining.

But please impress this conviction in my heart, so that Your hope will carry me through. I believe that You can heal me and so I entrust myself to You. Give me the graces I need to 'hang in there' until Your healing Love, which I know is constantly working on me, finally penetrates and gives me the relief that I need.

Amen.

Out of his infinite glory, may he give you
the power through his Spirit for your
hidden self to grow strong.

Ephesians 3:16

Prayer for Expectant Mothers

Lord,

I thank You for the gift of new life and especially for the child in my womb. I ask You to bless him or her so that the child will grow up in the way that You would wish. I also ask that my child will be healthy in every way and will grow to love You in his or her life.

I ask that You give me good health, especially during my pregnancy, and that You will see that all goes well for both of us during childbirth.

Amen.

For it was you who created my being,

knit me together in my mother's womb.

I thank you for the wonder

of my being.

Psalm 138/139:13–14

Prayer for Those who Long to Have a Child

Lord,

You know the deepest longings of my heart and how much I would love to have a child. I know every child is a gift from You, and so it is not something we can just demand. But You know that I would cherish that child so much and that I long to have the joy of giving life in this deep sense.

If it is your will, Lord, I ask You to bring our marriage to completion by giving us the gift of a child. If it is not Your will, give us the grace to accept what is Your will with love, and be Yourself the fullness of our love.

Amen.

O God, hear my cry!

Listen to my prayer.

Psalm 60/61:1

Prayer for Those with an Unplanned Pregnancy

Lord,

You know the fears that are in my heart just now, as I carry a child within me. You know I hadn't planned this and that I am really struggling. I beg You for Your grace to come to terms with the reality of it all. I know in my heart of hearts that each new life is a gift from You, to be cherished. Give me the grace to do just that, because I am finding it so hard just now.

Please support me with Your grace so that I keep firm in my resolution to keep this child. Give me the material support that I will need in order to do so and put the right people in my path to help me. Bless and protect the child in my womb, so that he or she will be healthy and grow up in Your care.

Amen.

Do not worry about tomorrow: tomorrow

will take care of itself. Each day has

enough trouble of its own.

Matthew 6:34

Prayer for Those Suffering Addictions

Lord,

You know the anguish that engulfs me. You have seen the spiral of horror in my life, the way my addiction consumes me and has taken over completely. You know I hate what I am doing to my family and friends, as they look on helplessly. It causes me such deep pain, and yet I seem to be totally unable to just kick the habit and start afresh.

Please, please help me. I seem to live for the 'high', but it is all so empty and meaningless and sometimes I just despair. Give me hope and the courage to change. Give my family the graces they need to cope. You have said that you came that we would have life to the full. Let me tap into the power that will help me to do that, Your Holy Spirit.

Amen.

For God, everything is possible.

Matthew 19:26

Prayer for Those in Financial Difficulty

Lord,

You know how difficult it is to make ends meet. Everything seems to be so expensive and it is a constant struggle.

Help me to have hope and provide for us so that I will be less consumed by this gnawing fear that is always with me. Help me to trust You to do this for us.

Amen.

We are in difficulties on all sides,

but never cornered;

we see no answer to our problems,

but never despair.

2 Corinthians 4:8

Prayer for Peace of Mind

O Jesus,

Banish from my mind all anxieties, troubles and fears of any kind. Make my mind calm and serene and fill it only with loving thoughts and confidence in You.

Amen.

When cares increase in my heart,

Your consolation calms my soul.

Psalm 93/94:19

Prayer for a Loving Marriage Partner

Heavenly Father,

The deepest desire of my heart is to meet someone with whom I can share love. I would really love to get married, to meet someone who could be a true soul-mate, someone I could love and cherish, as I wish to be loved myself.

It seems so hard today. People are afraid of commitment and, in truth, there is some fear in my own heart.

So I ask You, Lord, to grant this desire of my heart and let Your grace and love grow in me. I ask this in Jesus' name.

Amen.

If you find your delight in the Lord, He will grant you your heart's desire.

Psalm 36/37:4

Prayer for Those with Marital Difficulties

Heavenly Father,

I thank You for my marriage partner, for the gift of our married life together.

At this point in time, as You know, we are struggling. And it can be so painful at times – to be living so closely with someone and yet unable to communicate in a constructive way.

I ask You to come into the situation. You are the third person in our marriage and we need Your grace to continue on.

Let Your Spirit of love and reconciliation renew and deepen our love for each other and help us to grow in trust.

We ask this in Jesus' name.

Amen.

Love is always ready to excuse,
to trust, to hope and to endure
whatever comes.

1 Corinthians 13:7

Preparing for Exams

In exams, much depends on our performance over a period of a few intense hours. Keeping a calm mind is half the battle in recalling what we have studied and giving a good performance.

To be able to centre yourself for a few minutes before starting to study or even to stop for a brief pause is a great help. Even the few minutes sitting at the desk before the exam actually starts can be used profitably to become relaxed.

We offer the following exercise to help release the tension and calm the mind:

Close your eyes.

Take a few deep breaths. As you inhale, silently say, 'Come, Holy Spirit, inspire me.'

The Holy Spirit is the breath of God and the One who is the source of all our inspirations. As you pray this, imagine the Holy Spirit coming in to do this within you.

Exhaling slowly, silently say, 'Release the tension, bring your peace.'

As you pray this, feel the Holy Spirit drive the tension from your body.

This can be simplified to say 'Come, Holy Spirit' on inhalation and 'Bring your peace' on exhalation.

Prayer for Those Sitting Exams

Lord,

I ask You to help me at this stressful time. I feel that so much depends on these exams. I feel that in addition to carrying my own burdens, I am carrying the expectations of so many others – family, friends, society.

Help me to keep calm at this time, so that I can think straight and apply myself to the best of my ability. Let Your Spirit help and inspire me, so that I can remember all that I have studied and put together my answers in the best way. Guide me in all my ways, so that I will find fulfilment in You.

Amen.

Let Your good spirit guide me.

Psalm 142/143:10

Prayer for Students Taking Exams

Lord,

I ask you to send Your Spirit to inspire _____ in their studies. Help them to be attentive and alert. Help them to study the right topics. Inspire them during their actual exam so that they will stay calm and perform to the best of their ability.

I pray also that, in their quest for knowledge, they will come to know You and Your great love for them.

Amen.

There is nothing I cannot master

with the help of the One

who gives me strength.

Philippians 4:13

Final Prayer: to Experience God's Love for Us

As we conclude our reflections, we leave you with some words from the inaugural homily of Pope Benedict XVI.

Are we not perhaps all afraid in some way? If we let Christ enter fully into our lives, if we open ourselves totally to him, are we not afraid that He might take something away from us? Are we not perhaps afraid to give up something significant, something unique, something that makes life so beautiful? Do we not then risk ending up diminished and deprived of our freedom?

No! If we let Christ into our lives, we lose nothing, nothing, absolutely nothing of what makes life free, beautiful and great. No! Only in this friendship are the doors of life opened wide.

Do not be afraid of Christ! He takes nothing away and He gives you everything. When we give ourselves to Him, we receive a hundredfold in return. Yes, open, open wide the doors to Christ – and you will find true life.

Amen.

We hope that this book has given you a way of coming closer to the Lord. We hope that you will come to experience, in a full and deep way, God's all-embracing love for you. A prayer that beautifully expresses the fullness that is possible was written by St Paul, found in the third chapter of the letter to the Ephesians. This is our prayer for you:

This, then, is what I pray, kneeling before the Father,
from whom every family, whether spiritual
or natural, takes its name.

Out of His infinite glory, may He give you the power
through His Spirit for your hidden self to grow strong,
so that Christ may live in your hearts through faith, and
then, planted in love and built on love, you will with all
the saints have the strength to grasp the breadth and
the length, the height and the depth; until, knowing the
love of Christ, which is beyond all knowledge, you are
filled with the utter fullness of God.

Glory be to Him, whose power, working in us, can do
infinitely more than we can ask or imagine.

Amen.

May the Lord bless you and keep you.

May He show His face to you and have mercy on you.

May He turn His countenance to you and

give peace to you.

The Blessing of St Clare

Further
Reading and
Reflections

Scripture for Reflection

Realise that God is speaking to you in His Word. Jesus is the Word of God. Ask the Holy Spirit to open your heart so that you may truly hear God speak to you. It is preferable to pray these words aloud, so that they may sink deep within you. And pray them with faith, knowing that God is God and is Lord of all.

Scripture Quotations for Life

Come to Me, all you who labour

and are overburdened and I will

give you rest.

Matthew 11:28–30

Fresh and green are the pastures

Where He gives me repose

Near restful waters He leads me

to revive my drooping spirits.

Psalm 22/23:2–3

Do not be afraid, for I have redeemed

you. I have called you by your name;

you are Mine.

Isaiah 43:1

You are my hiding place, O Lord;

You save me from distress,

You surround me with cries of deliverance.

Psalm 31/32:7

Commit your life to the Lord,

trust in Him and He will act.

Psalm 36/37:5

I am going to lure her and will lead her

out into the wilderness and speak

to her heart.

Hosea 2:14

She, the faithful one,

whose mind is steadfast,

who keeps the peace,

because she trusts in you.

Isaiah 26:2–3

We know that by turning everything to
their good, God co-operates with all those
who love Him, with all those that He has
called according to his purpose.

Romans 8:28

Sufferings bring patience, as we know,

and patience brings perseverance,

and perseverance brings hope,

and this hope is not deceptive,

because the love of God

has been poured into our hearts by the

Holy Spirit which has been given us.

Romans 5:3–5

I have loved You with an everlasting love,

so I am constant in my affection for You.

Jeremiah 31:3

When you seek Me you shall find Me,

when you seek Me with all your heart.

I will let you find Me.

Jeremiah 29:13–14

Courage, get up; He is calling you.

Mark 10:50

Peace I bequeath to you,

My own peace I give you,

a peace the world cannot give,

this is My gift to you.

Do not let your hearts be troubled or afraid.

John 14:27

1 shall give you a new heart and put

a new spirit in you.

Ezekiel 36:26

My grace is enough for you:
My power is at its best in weakness.

2 Corinthians 12:9

Fill your minds with everything that is true,

everything that is noble,

everything that is good and pure,

everything that we love and honour,

and everything that can be thought

virtuous or worthy of praise.

Then the God of peace will be with you.

Philippians 4:8–9

1 know the plans I have in mind for you –

it is Yahweh who speaks –

plans for peace, not disaster,

reserving a future full of hope for you.

Jeremiah 29:11, 13

Jesus said, 'I have come so that they may have life and have it to the full.'

John 10:10

At night there are tears,

but joy comes with dawn.

Psalm 29/30:5

Cast your burden on the Lord and He will sustain you.

Psalm 54/55:22

If anyone wants to be a follower of Mine,

let him renounce himself and take up his

cross and follow Me.

Matthew 16:24

'Lord, how often should I forgive my brother if he wrongs me? As often as seven times?' Jesus answered, 'Not seven, I tell you, but seventy-seven times.'

Matthew 18:21–22

I am the good shepherd; I know My own

and My own know me.

John 10:14

If your lips confess that Jesus is Lord, and if

you believe in your heart that God raised

Him from the dead,

then you will be saved.

Romans 10:9

Since he clings to me in love, I will free

him, protect him for he knows my name.

When he calls I shall answer:

'I am with you.' I will save him in

distress and give him glory.

Psalm 90/91:14–15

In God alone is my soul at rest.

Psalm 62/63:1

Psalm 138–139

O Lord, You search me and You know me,
You know my resting and my rising,
You discern my purpose from afar.
You mark when I walk or lie down,
all my ways lie open to You.
Before ever a word is on my tongue
You know it, O Lord, through and through.
Behind and before You besiege me,
Your hand ever laid upon me.
Too wonderful for me this knowledge,
too high, beyond my reach.
O where can I go from Your spirit,
or where can I flee from Your face?
If I climb the heavens, You are there.
If I lie in the grave, You are there.
If I take the wings of the dawn
and dwell at the sea's farthest end,

even there Your hand would lead me,
Your right hand would hold me fast.
If I say: 'Let the darkness hide me
and the light around me be night',
even darkness is not dark for You
and the night is as clear as the day.

For it was You who created my being,
knit me together in my mother's womb.
I thank You for the wonder of my being,
for the wonders of all Your creation.
Already You knew my soul,
my body held no secret from You
when I was being fashioned in secret
and moulded in the depths of the earth.
Your eyes saw all my actions,
they were all of them written in Your book;
every one of my days was decreed
before one of them came into being.

To me, how mysterious Your thoughts,
the sum of them not to be numbered!
If I count them, they are more than the sand;
to finish, I must be eternal, like You.
O search me, God, and know my heart.
O test me and know my thoughts.
See that I follow not the wrong path
and lead me in the path of life eternal.

Contemplation

The following are reflections on contemplation based on the writings of José Rodriguez Carballo OFM, Minister General.

We suggest taking one at a time into your prayer and letting them sink into your spirit.

Contemplation is ...

… an openness of the heart to the mystery that

envelops us, so that we may be possessed by it.

Contemplation is ...

… emptying ourselves of the superfluous,

so that He who is All may fill us to overflowing.

Contemplation is ...

… opening wide the eyes of the heart, in order to

read and discover the presence of the Lord deep

inside people and things.

Contemplation is ...

... creating silence so that our gaze,

expressive of awesome wonder,

may speak like the gaze of a child does:

our hands, ready for service, may speak

like those of a mother;

our feet may speak by being ready to walk

in haste – as St Clare asked us – and

cross borders to proclaim the Good News

like missionaries;

and our hearts, passionate for both Christ

and humanity, may speak as the hearts of

both St Francis and St Clare who were

in love with God.

205

Contemplation is ...

... entering the cell of your heart and, through an indwelling silence, allowing yourself to be transformed by Him whom, like St Clare, we confess as the spouse of a more noble lineage (1 LAg 7); whose appearance is the most beautiful (1 LAg 9); whose beauty all the blessed hosts of the heavens unceasingly admire (4 LAg 10); and whose affection moves (4 LAg 11).

Contemplation is ...

... to opt exclusively for the Lord, giving Him our life: it is being able to say with Paul, I live, but not I; it is Christ living in me (Galatians 2:20). It has nothing to do with a mediocre, monotonous and weary way of life.

Contemplation is ...

... giving of yourself totally to Him who has given

Himself totally to us (Lt Ord 29).

Contemplation is ...

… caring for others, because being passionate

for Christ and being passionate for humanity

go hand in hand.

Reflections on the Rosary by Blessed John Paul II

'The Rosary', precisely because it starts with Mary's own experience, is an exquisitely contemplative prayer. Without this contemplative dimension, it would lose its meaning, as Pope Paul VI clearly pointed out:

> *Without contemplation, the Rosary is a body without a soul, and its recitation runs the risk of becoming a mechanical repetition of formulas, in violation of the admonition of Christ: 'In praying do not heap up empty phrases as the Gentiles do; for they think they will be heard for their many words' (Matthew 6:7). By its nature the recitation of the Rosary calls for a quiet rhythm and a lingering pace, helping the individual to meditate on the mysteries of the Lord's life as seen through the eyes of her who was closest to the Lord. In this way, the unfathomable riches of these mysteries are disclosed.*

It is worth pausing to consider this profound insight of Pope Paul VI, in order to bring out certain aspects of the Rosary which show that it is really a form of Christocentric contemplation (RVM 14).

With regard to praying for peace and for our families, Blessed John Paul II has the following to say:

As a prayer for peace, the Rosary is also, and always has been, a prayer of and for the family – the family that prays together stays together.

The Holy Rosary, by age-old tradition, has shown itself particularly effective as a prayer that brings the family together. Individual family members, in turning their eyes towards Jesus, also regain the ability to look one another in the eye, to communicate, to show solidarity, to forgive one another and to see their covenant of love renewed in the Spirit of God.

Many of the problems facing contemporary families, especially in economically developed societies, result from their increasing difficulty in communicating. Families seldom manage to come together, and the rare occasions when they do are often taken up with watching television. To return to the recitation of the family Rosary means filling daily life with very different images, images of the mystery of salvation: the image of the Redeemer, the image of His most Blessed Mother. The family that recites the Rosary together reproduces something of the atmosphere of

the household of Nazareth: its members place Jesus at the centre, they share His joys and sorrows, they place their needs and their plans in His hands, they draw from Him the hope and the strength to go on. (RVM 41)

On Healing

A reflection on healing by
Bishop Martin Drennan, Bishop of Galway

Seeing their faith, Jesus said to the paralytic, '*My child, your sins are forgiven.*' He continued, '*I order you: get up, pick up your stretcher and go off home.*' And the man got up, picked up his stretcher at once and walked out in front of everyone (Mark 2:1–12).

When we come to meet God in prayer, our hope is that we will return home changed, transformed, by that meeting. Our gospel passage invites us to pause and consider that process of transformation in the setting of the Sunday Eucharist. Four elements are singled out – in faith, we come to the Lord's presence, we hear His Word that forgives, we hear His Word that heals our paralysis, we return home saying that God is great.

When we come to the Lord, we carry people in our hearts. Like the four men who are mentioned in today's gospel, we carry people into the Lord's Presence in faith and let Him surprise them with His Words of forgiveness and healing. Others carry us into God's presence to ask His blessings on us. He speaks His Words of forgiveness so that we may be less unworthy in His presence. What happens is put strongly by the prophet Isaiah, '*I, I am He who blots out your transgressions for my own sake, and I will not remember your sins*' (Isaiah 43:25). We may find it difficult to forget our sins, others may remember them, but God forgets them. So, we don't need to carry the past with shame or guilt. In His mercy, God releases us from what makes us immobile.

His Word heals our paralysis. For that healing to be effective, we need to name accurately what is paralysing us. Normally, hidden diseases are not cured. The disease that is named may require great skills in those seeking to cure it, but there is no effective way of dealing with what isn't named. When 'hurt' is properly named as 'anger', it is actually easier to look at how to deal with it. There are many pain points that paralyse – unhealed relationships, mistakes, jealousy, envy, greed, prejudice, cynicism,

shame, guilt, anxiety and fear. God asks that we be present to Him now. However, we can get stuck in events or memories from the past that caused pain. If pain from the past is not transformed, then we pass it on. Jesus wants to touch our pain points and heal them. Words have the power to console and bring peace. His Word is always good news, a word that guides us into the way of peace.

Those who witnessed the cure of the paralytic were astonished. They knew that God was the source of the miracle and directed their praise to Him. The aim of the Sunday Eucharist is to send us home saying that God is great. The choir may have been magnificent and maybe the preacher too, but it is to God first and foremost that our praise is to be given. He has done so much for us, given so much, constantly cares so much, that the only fitting response is thanksgiving, wonder at His goodness.

For Prayer on Healing

Is the word of God helping me to identify
the areas of paralysis in my life?

If my prayer for healing is not effective, it
might be because it is too vague, not
precise enough in naming what I desire
from the Lord.

Is the Eucharist gradually forming me
into a person of thanksgiving?

Sources and Abbreviations

The authors and publisher would like to thank the following for permission to reproduce text and quotations:

'The Surrender Prayer' is reproduced with permission from The Fr Walter Ciszek Prayer League, Inc., 231 North Jardin Street, Shenandoah, PA 17976, USA.

Extract from Silvester O'Flynn OFM Cap, *The Good News of Mark's Year.* (Dublin: Columba Press, 1990).

Extract from Fr Walter Ciszek, *He Leadeth Me* (New York, Doubleday, 1973).

All quotations from the Psalms are taken from the Grail version, which is used in the Divine Office.

All other scripture quotations taken from the Jerusalem Bible.

Quotations from St Francis are taken from Regis J. Armstrong, *Francis of Assisi: Early Documents – The Saint* (New York: New City Press, 1999).

Quotations from St Clare are taken from Regis J. Armstrong, *St Clare of Assisi: Early Documents – The Lady* (New York: New City Press, 2006).

CCC   Catechism of the Catholic Church

RVM   Rosarium Virginis Mariae

1 LAg   First letter to St Agnes of Prague

2 LAg   Second letter to St Agnes of Prague

3 LAg   Third letter to St Agnes of Prague

4 LAg   Fourth letter to St Agnes of Prague

Bl C   Blessing of St Clare

PC   Acts of the Process of Canonisation of St Clare

L Cl   Legend of St Clare

Lt Ord   A letter to the Entire Order

Ct Exh   Canticle of Exhortation for the Ladies of San Damiano

Acknowledgements

For the immediate help that we have had in putting this book together, we want to thank especially our editor Ciara Doorley, who has been so helpful during this process. We also wish to thank all at Hachette Ireland and Noel Cassidy, the graphic designer, who has done a great job and everyone else who has helped us bring this book to fruition.

We have been deeply conscious of how we have been supported in so many ways in writing this book. As we live on Divine Providence, we are constantly in a position of expressing gratitude. The reality of our life is that we would not be here if we were not supported by the people of Galway, primarily, but also by a much wider extended family.

For this we are extremely grateful to those who help us in big ways as well as small. We hope that the book is a fruit of our way of life here and so we dedicate it to all those, known and unknown, who have always been there for us. This book is for you.

The Poor Clares
Nuns' Island
Galway
Ireland